ABOVE ALL

- PIANO LEVEL -
LATE INTERMEDIATE/EARLY ADVANCED

Cover Photo: Jean Schroedl

ISBN 978-0-634-06344-2

7777 W. BLUEMOUND RD. P.O. BOX 13819 MILWAUKEE, WI 53213

Visit Hal Leonard Online at
www.halleonard.com
Visit Phillip at
www.phillipkeveren.com

PREFACE

To my musical friends,

This collection of arrangements was written during a particularly interesting season in my family's life. I wrote the first few arrangements while enjoying the springtime of Southern California, our home for the past 22 years. During those decades I married my wife, Lisa. It was in those sunny surroundings that our children Lindsay and Sean came into the world. This summer we moved to Tennessee, and it was here in the lush green beauty of our new hometown that I completed these arrangements.

With the upheaval of a cross-country move, one becomes more aware of the transitory nature of our lives. Things change; life moves in new directions; nothing is forever…except the never-changing love of God! These songs speak of that timeless truth, and I hope they minister to you as they have to me.

With best wishes,
Phillip Keveren

BIOGRAPHY

Phillip Keveren, a multi-talented keyboard artist and composer, has composed original works in a variety of genres from piano solo to symphonic orchestra. Mr. Keveren gives frequent concerts and workshops for teachers and their students in the United States, Canada, Europe, and Asia. Mr. Keveren holds a B.M. in composition from California State University Northridge and a M.M. in composition from the University of Southern California.

CONTENTS

ABOVE ALL

Words and Music by Paul Baloche and Lenny LeBlanc

Above all powers, above all kings,
Above all nature and all created things;
Above all wisdom and all the ways of man,
You were here before the world began.

Above all kingdoms, above all thrones,
Above all wonders the world has ever known;
Above all wealth and treasures of the earth,
There's no way to measure what You're worth.

Crucified, laid behind a stone,
You lived to die rejected and alone.
Like a rose trampled on the ground,
You took the fall and thought of me above all.

This has one of the most meaningful lyrics of any worship song I know. It is poetic, yet in a way that speaks directly to the contemporary church. I find the music to be beautiful, and it works wonderfully as an instrumental solo. I have no doubt that this song will touch many generations to come.

PK

ABOVE ALL

Words and Music by PAUL BALOCHE
and LENNY LeBLANC
Arranged by Phillip Keveren

Slowly, worshipfully ($\quarternote = 60$)

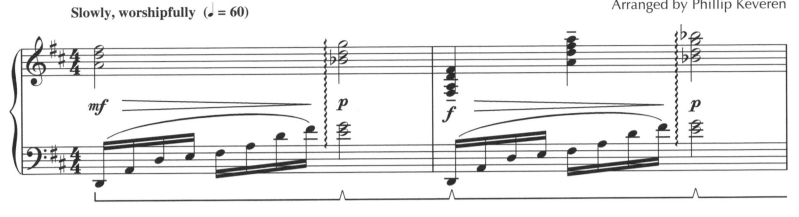

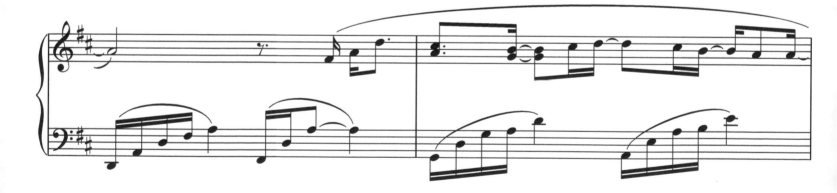

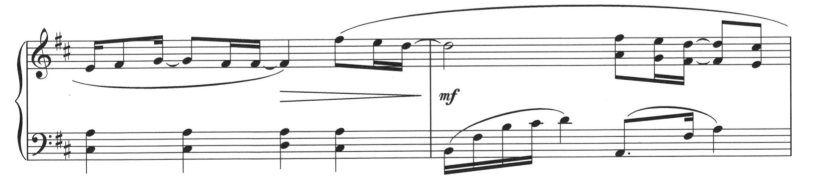

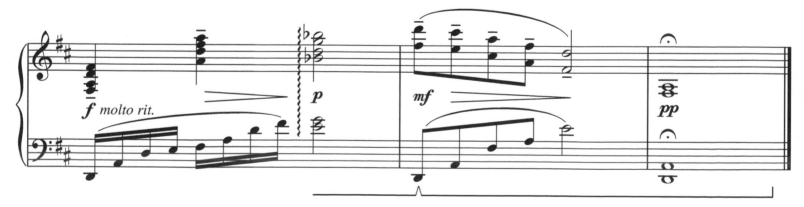

ANCIENT OF DAYS

Words and Music by Gary Sadler and Jamie Harvill

Blessing and honor, glory and power
Be unto the Ancient of Days.
From ev'ry nation, all of creation,
Bow before the Ancient of Days.

Ev'ry tongue in heaven and earth shall declare Your glory.
Ev'ry knee shall bow at Your throne in worship.
You will be exalted, O God,
And Your kingdom shall not pass away,
O Ancient of Days.

Your kingdom shall reign over all the earth.
Sing unto the Ancient of Days.
For none can compare to Your matchless worth.
Sing unto the Ancient of Days.

This chorus has been set in a "classical" style and would be effective as a postlude due to its fanfare-like qualities. My worship team in California loved this song, and we sang it often. Although we played it in a pop/rock style, it always seemed to me that it would work well in a stately arrangement.

PK

ANCIENT OF DAYS

Words and Music by GARY SADLER
and JAMIE HARVILL
Arranged by Phillip Keveren

Stately (♩ = 112)

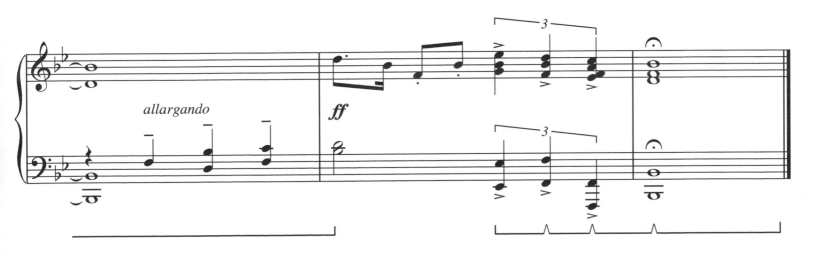

AGNUS DEI

Words and Music by Michael W. Smith

Alleluia, Alleluia,
For the Lord God Almighty reigns.
Alleluia, Alleluia,
For the Lord God Almighty reigns.
Alleluia.

Holy, holy are You, Lord God Almighty.
Worthy is the Lamb, worthy is the Lamb.
You are holy, holy are You, Lord God Almighty.
Worthy is the Lamb, worthy is the Lamb. Amen.

The opening section of this arrangement captures the ethereal nature of Michael W. Smith's composition. Play this with great freedom. The with motion *tempo establishes an original ostinato pattern over which the theme continues to develop. This material should flow gracefully.*

PK

AGNUS DEI

Words and Music by
MICHAEL W. SMITH
Arranged by Phillip Keveren

With mystery, rubato

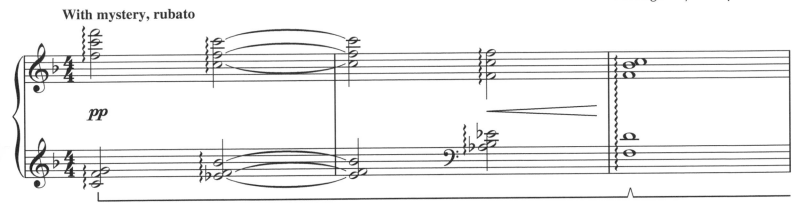

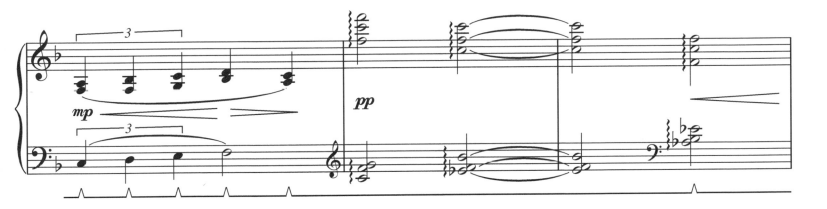

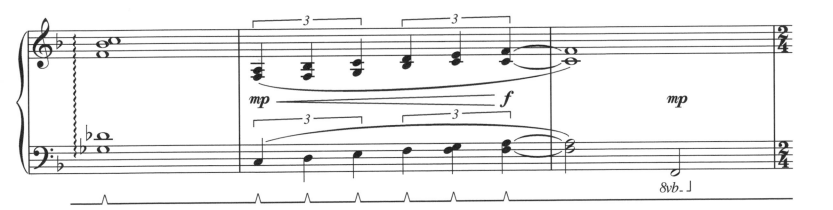

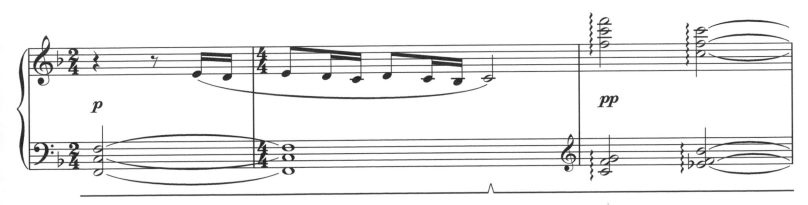

With motion ($\quarternote$ = 82 - 86)

sub. **p**

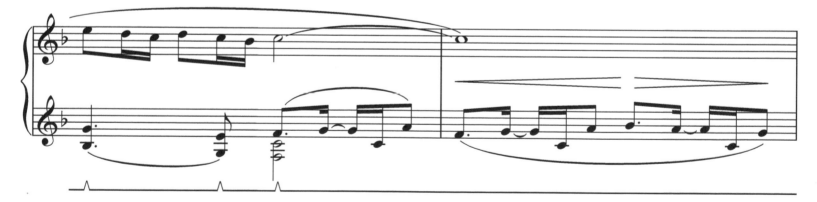

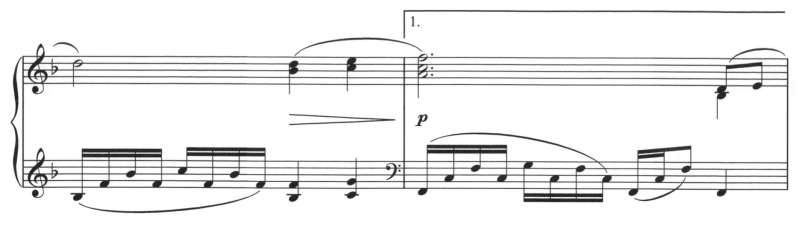

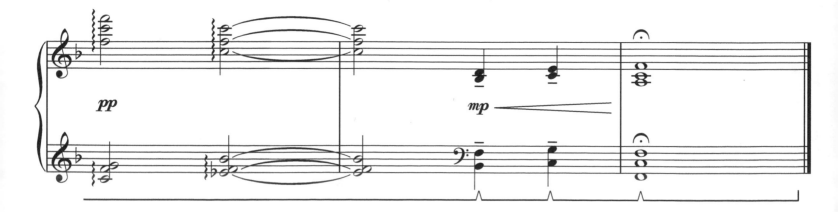

CREATE IN ME A CLEAN HEART

Words and Music by Keith Green

Create in me a clean heart, O God,
And renew a right spirit within me.
Cast me not away from Thy presence, O Lord,
And take not Thy Holy Spirit from me.
Restore unto me the joy of Thy salvation,
And renew a right spirit within me.

This chorus has been a blessing to worshipping congregations for quite some time now. In my experience, it is often played with a country flavor. A Mozartian mood makes this setting a bit unique.

PK

CREATE IN ME A CLEAN HEART

Words and Music by
KEITH GREEN
Arranged by Phillip Keveren

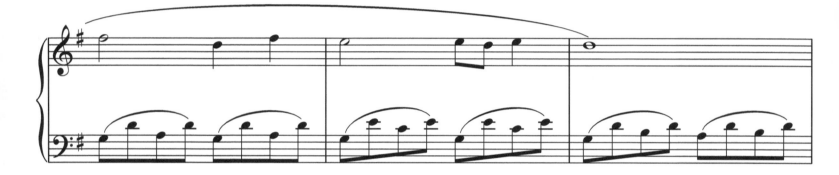

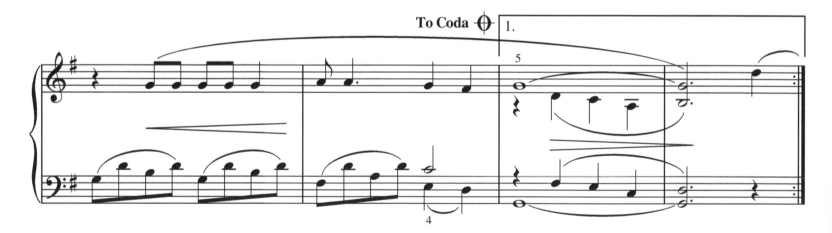

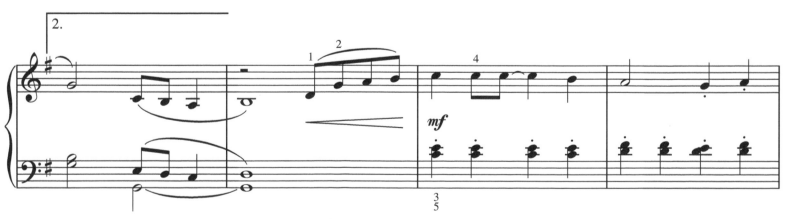

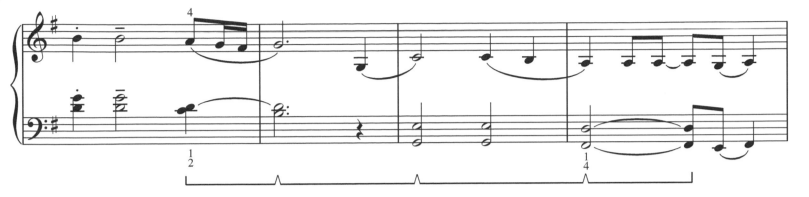

D.S. al Coda

CODA

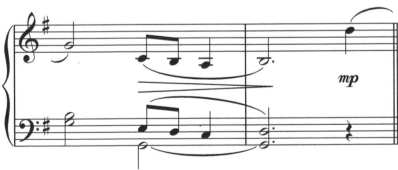

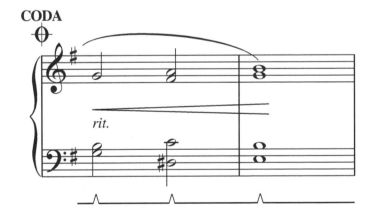

Slower

BREATHE

Words and Music by Marie Barnett

This is the air I breathe,
This is the air I breathe,
Your holy presence living in me.

And I, I'm desp'rate for You.
And I, I'm lost without You.
Oh, Lord, I'm lost without You.
I'm lost without You, and You are my daily bread.

This is my daily bread,
This is my daily bread,
Your very Word spoken to me.

And I, I'm desp'rate for You.
And I, I'm lost without You.
Oh, Lord, I'm lost without You.
I'm lost without You, I'm nothing without You.

This song has a peaceful serenity about it that makes it a favorite of mine. Don't get in a rush. Let it spin out in an unhurried manner. I tend to take it somewhat faster at the key change and then drop back to the original tempo at the D.S.

PK

BREATHE

Words and Music by
MARIE BARNETT
Arranged by Phillip Keveren

Gently (♩ = 80)

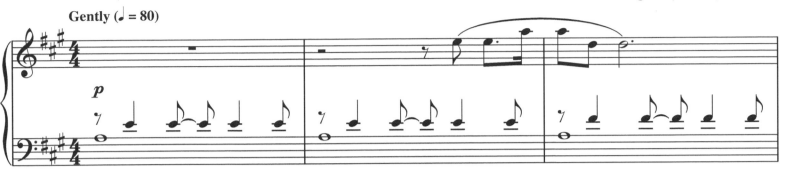

With pedal

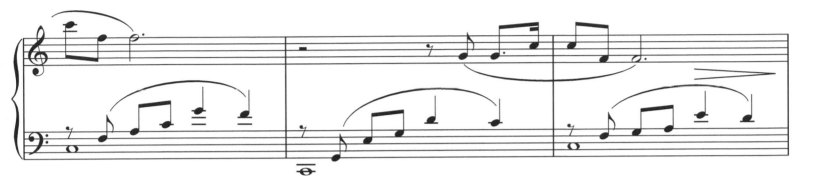

D.S. al Coda

CODA

COME, NOW IS THE TIME TO WORSHIP

Words and Music by Brian Doerkson

Come, now is the time to worship.
Come, now is the time to give your heart.
Come, just as you are, to worship.
Come, just as you are, before your God.
Come.

One day ev'ry tongue will confess You are God.
One day ev'ry knee will bow.
Still, the greatest treasure remains for those
Who gladly choose You now.

Ooh, we're calling You.
Calling all nations:
Now is the time.

I recall first hearing this song on the radio. The presentation was simply guitar and voice, and the performance was deeply moving. I tried to keep this arrangement rather straight-forward, evoking the reverence I sensed in that initial hearing.

PK

COME, NOW IS THE TIME TO WORSHIP

Words and Music by
BRIAN DOERKSON
Arranged by Phillip Keveren

With pedal

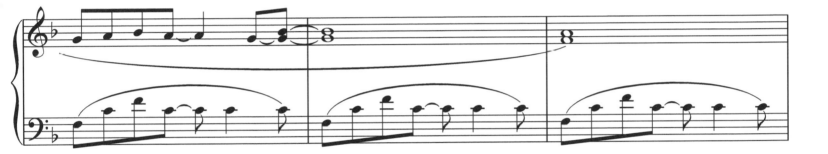

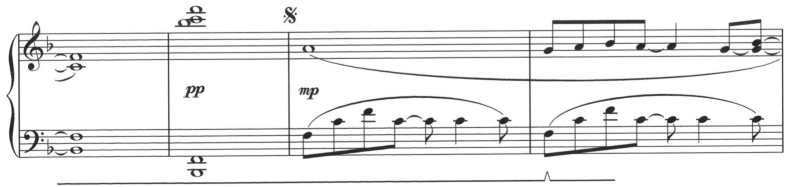

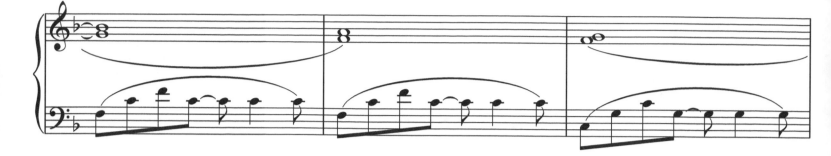

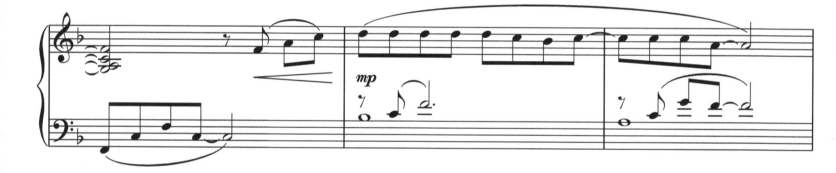

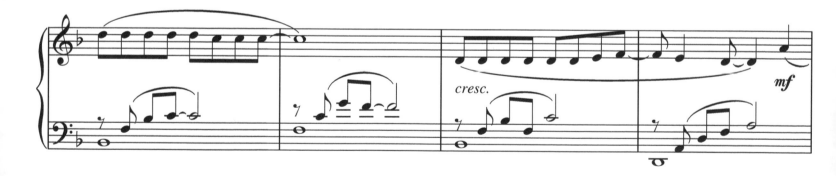

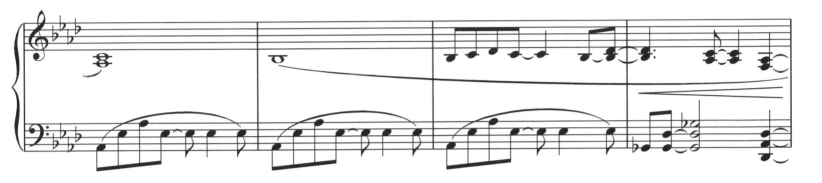

D.S. al Coda

CODA

DRAW ME CLOSE

Words and Music by Kelly Carpenter

Draw me close to You,
Never let me go.
I lay it all down again, O Lord,
To hear You say that I'm Your friend.
You are my desire, no one else will do,
'Cause nothing else can take Your place, oh, no, no,
To feel the warmth of Your embrace.
Help me find the way,
Bring me back to You.
Bring me back, oh, Jesus, yeah.

You're all I want.
You're all I've ever needed.
You're all I want.
Help me know You are near.

Although I had heard this song prior to Michael W. Smith's recent recording, it was his rendition that really brought it to my attention. A sweeping melody combined with a powerful lyric make this composition memorable. Keep the left hand light in the verses so the right hand melody can sing out effortlessly.

PK

DRAW ME CLOSE

Words and Music by
KELLY CARPENTER
Arranged by Phillip Keveren

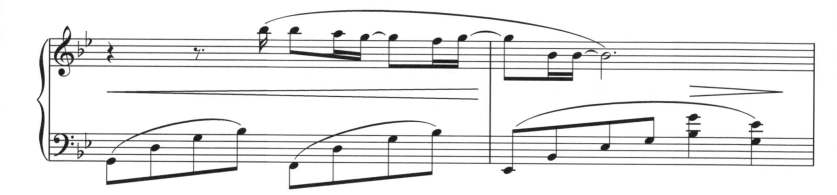

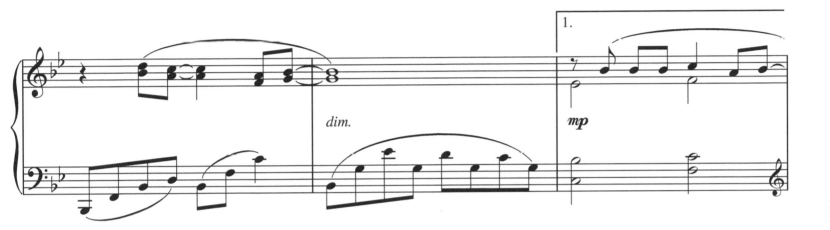

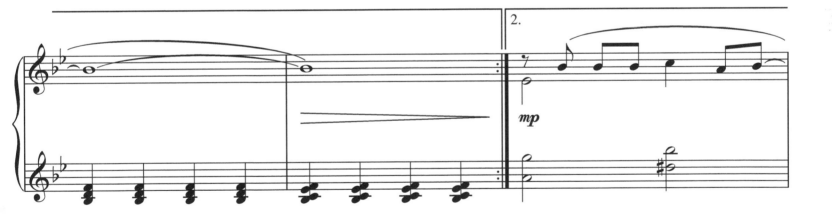

HE IS EXALTED

Words and Music by Twila Paris

He is exalted,
The King is exalted on high,
I will praise Him.
He is exalted,
Forever exalted,
And I will praise His name!
He is the Lord,
Forever His truth shall reign.
Heaven and earth
Rejoice in His holy name.
He is exalted,
The King is exalted on high!

Twila Paris' classic song is one that I have used as an instrumental solo for many years. At a brisk, energetic tempo it serves well as a prelude or postlude.

PK

HE IS EXALTED

Words and Music by
TWILA PARIS
Arranged by Phillip Keveren

Briskly (♩. = 66-72)

Pedal lightly

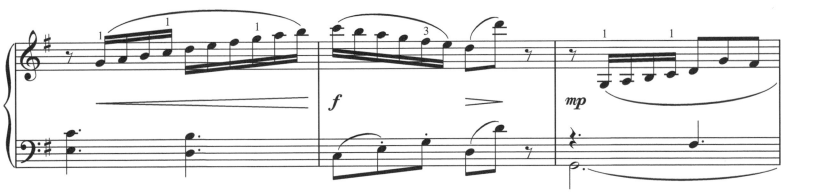

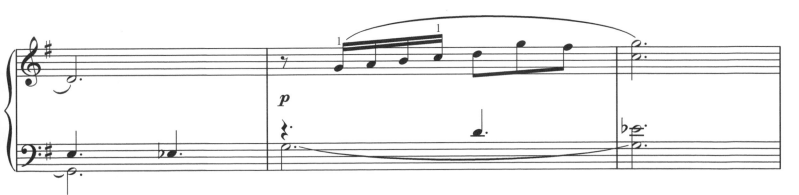

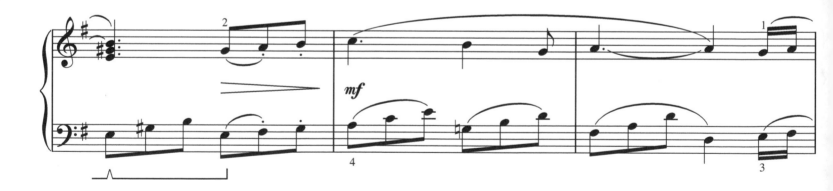

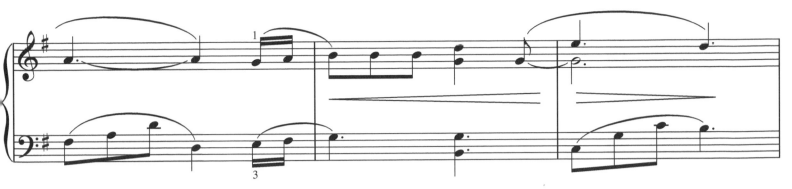

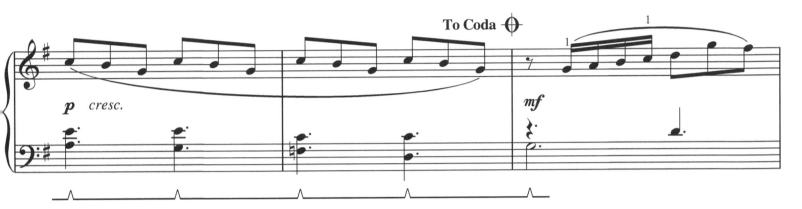

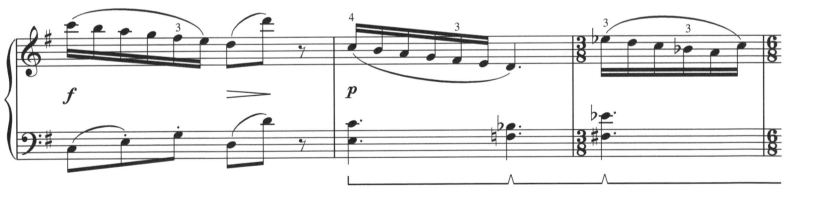

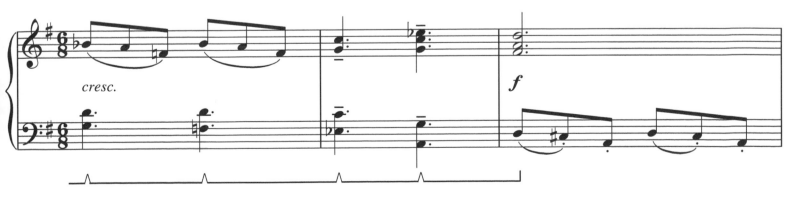

D.S. al Coda

allargando   **ff** *a tempo*

CODA

ff   *L.H. over R.H.*

molto rit.

LAMB OF GOD

Words and Music by Twila Paris

Your only Son, no sin to hide,
But You have sent Him from Your side
To walk upon this guilty sod
And to become the Lamb of God.

Your gift of Love they crucified,
They laughed and scorned Him as He died.
The humble King they named a fraud
And sacrificed the Lamb of God.

CHORUS:
Oh, Lamb of God, sweet Lamb of God,
I love the holy Lamb of God.
Oh, wash me in His precious blood,
My Jesus Christ, the Lamb of God.

I was so lost, I should have died,
But You have brought me to Your side
To be led by Your staff and rod
And to be called the Lamb of God.

CHORUS

A melody with the lilt of an Irish folk tune, this poignant song has found an enduring home in the music of the Christian faith. I have heard it sung in a variety of styles, but it really doesn't matter. The melody and lyric rise up and stir a listener in whatever setting. This arrangement should be played spaciously, with lyrical, tender phrasing.

PK

LAMB OF GOD

Words and Music by
TWILA PARIS
Arranged by Phillip Keveren

Slowly, tenderly

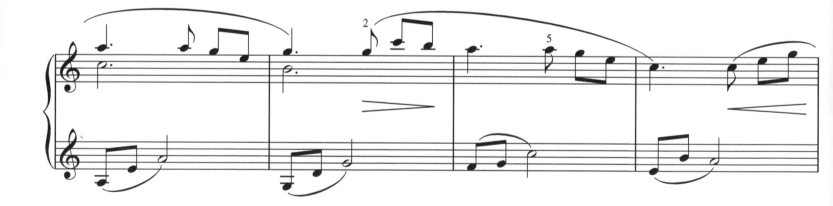

I STAND IN AWE

Words and Music by Mark Altrogge

You are beautiful beyond description,
Too marvelous for words,
Too wonderful for comprehension,
Like nothing ever seen or heard.
Who can grasp Your infinite wisdom?
Who can fathom the depth of Your love?
You are beautiful beyond description,
Majesty enthroned above.

And I stand, I stand in awe of You.
I stand, I stand in awe of You.
Holy God, to whom all praise is due,
I stand in awe of You.

I love both the verse and chorus to this composition. The verse is sweet and gentle, while the chorus takes on a more majestic character. Allow the ending of this arrangement to drift away, leaving the listener wondering for a moment if it's really over…

PK

I STAND IN AWE

Words and Music by
MARK ALTROGGE
Arranged by Phillip Keveren

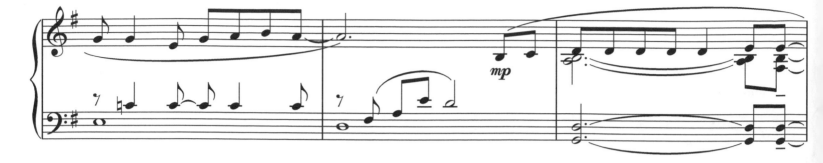

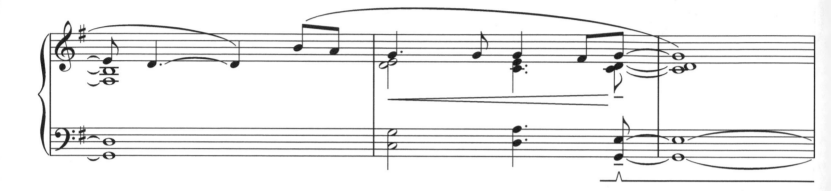

I WANT TO KNOW YOU

Words and Music by Andy Park

In the secret, in the quiet place,
In the stillness You are there.
In the secret, in the quiet hour I wait only for You,
'Cause I want to know You more.

CHORUS:
I want to know You,
I want to hear Your voice.
I want to know You more.
I want to touch You,
I want to see Your face.
I want to know You more.

I am reaching for the highest goal,
That I might receive the prize.
Pressing onward, pushing ev'ry hindrance aside, out of my way,
'Cause I want to know You more.

CHORUS

A truly wonderful song that sounds equally beautiful in a spirited or tranquil mood. I chose to place the melody in a jazz harmonic environment. It should be played slowly and very freely, with a sense of wonder.

PK

I WANT TO KNOW YOU

Words and Music by
ANDY PARK
Arranged by Phillip Keveren

Rubato, serenely

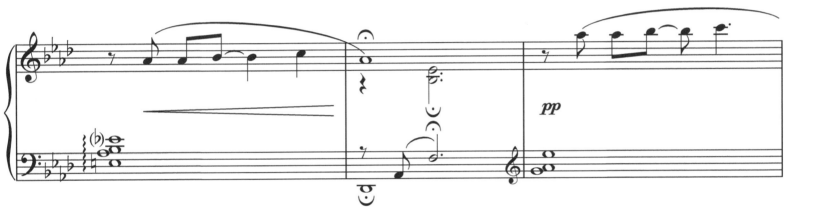

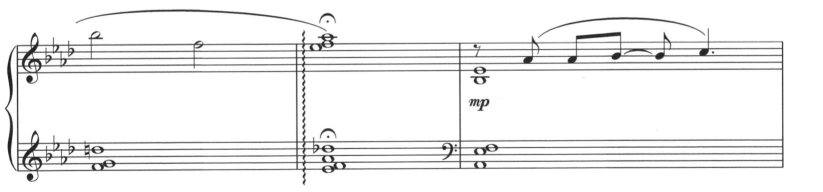

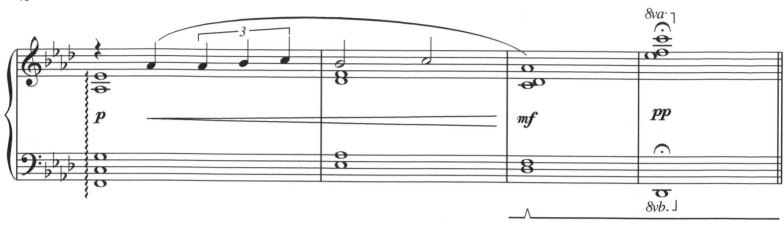

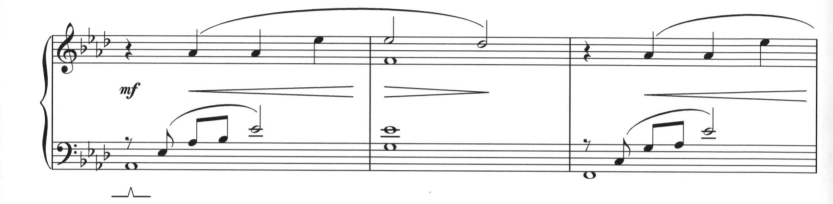

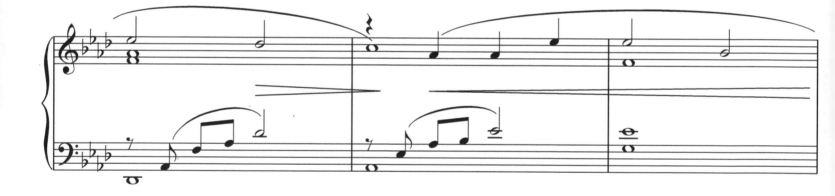

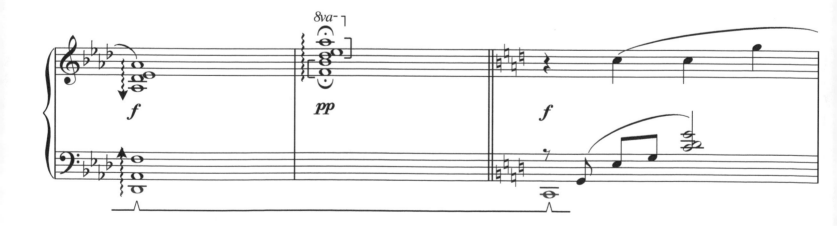

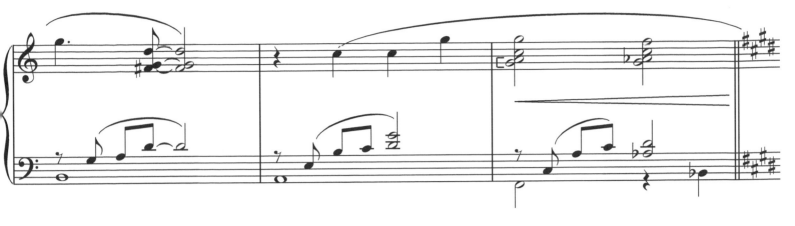

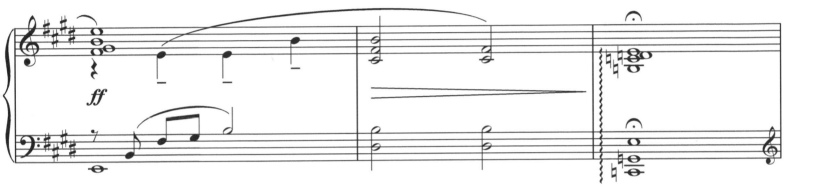

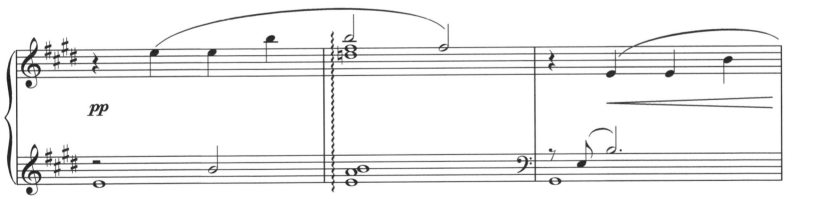

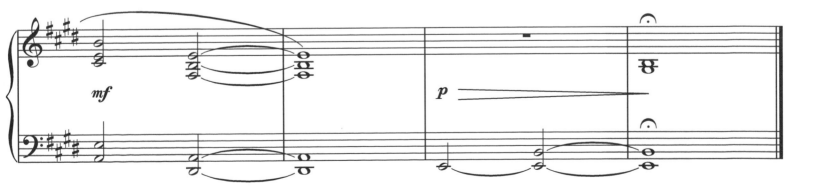

MORE LOVE, MORE POWER

Words and Music by Jude Del Hierro

More love, more power,
More of You in my life.
More love, more power,
More of You in my life.
And I will worship You with all of my heart,
And I will worship You with all of my mind,
And I will worship You with all of my strength,
For You are my Lord.

And I will sing Your praise with all of my heart,
And I will sing Your praise with all of my mind,
And I will sing Your praise with all of my strength,
For You are my Lord.

Bittersweet minor harmony makes this chorus special. I have been amazed at how lovely this chorus sounds with a congregation singing in a soft unison. Let this arrangement build slowly, being careful not to give too much away too soon.

PK

MORE LOVE, MORE POWER

Words and Music by
JUDE DEL HIERRO
Arranged by Phillip Keveren

Slowly, freely

With pedal

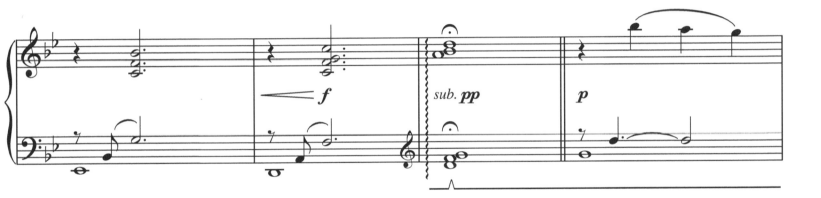

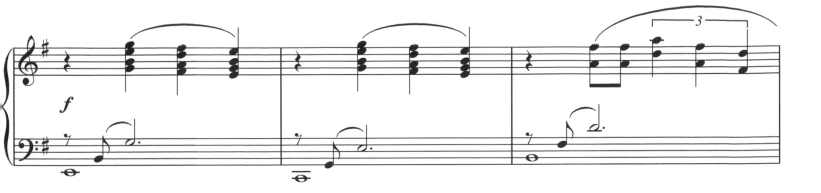

WE FALL DOWN

Words and Music by Chris Tomlin

We fall down, we lay our crowns at the feet of Jesus,
The greatness of mercy and love at the feet of Jesus.
And we cry, "Holy, holy, holy,"
And we cry, "Holy, holy, holy,"
And we cry, "Holy, holy, holy is the Lamb."

This is a meaningful song to me. I wanted the arrangement to unfold in a peaceful, worshipful manner. I tend to play it somewhat rubato until the left hand begins the steady eighth-note pattern at the chorus.

PK

WE FALL DOWN

Words and Music by
CHRIS TOMLIN
Arranged by Phillip Keveren

Worshipfully (♩ = 76)

With pedal

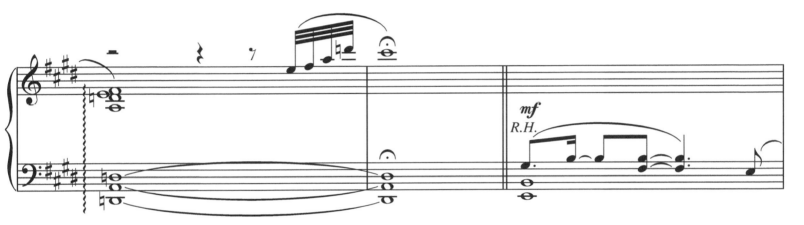

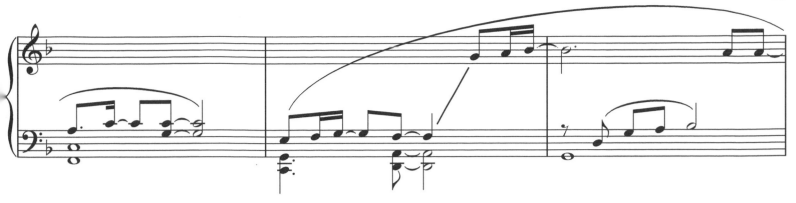

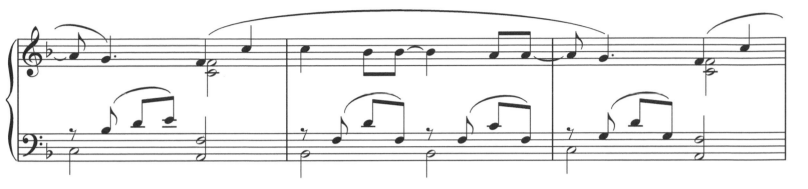

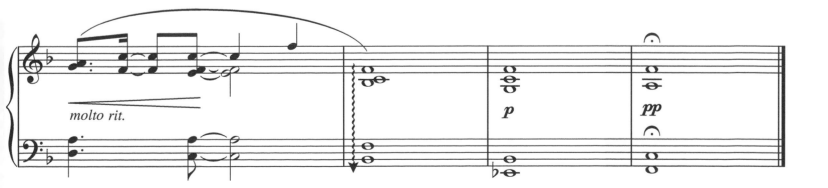

YOU ARE MY KING (AMAZING LOVE)

Words and Music by Billy James Foote

I'm forgiven because You were forsaken.
I'm accepted, You were condemned.
I'm alive and well, Your spirit is within me
Because You died and rose again.

Amazing love, how can it be
That You, my King would die for me?
Amazing love, and I know it's true,
It's my joy to honor You.
In all I do, I honor You.

You are my King.
You are my King.
Jesus, You are my King.
Jesus, You are my King.

Here is a song that I first heard through my children's youth group. I tried to create an impressionistic setting of this tune. Pedal liberally and let it flow gracefully.

PK

YOU ARE MY KING
(Amazing Love)

Words and Music by
BILLY JAMES FOOTE
Arranged by Phillip Keveren

Flowing (♩ = 78)

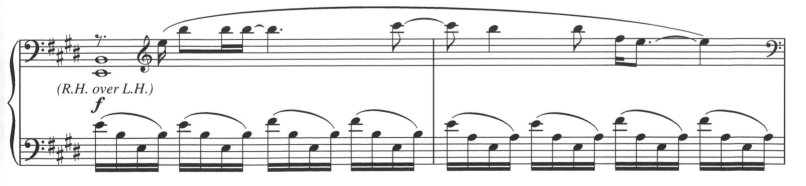

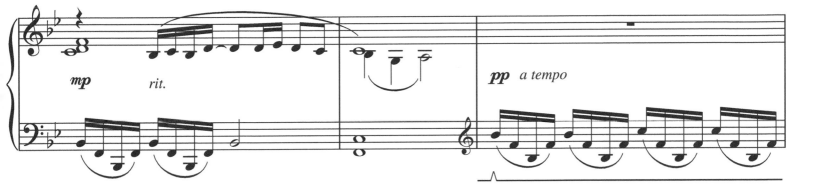

STEP BY STEP

Words and Music by David Strasser

O God, You are my God,
And I will ever praise You.
O God, You are my God,
And I will ever praise You.
I will seek You in the morning,
And I will learn to walk in Your ways.
And step by step You'll lead me,
And I will follow You all of my days.

This arrangement is built around the driving syncopated rhythm that opens the piece. I am imagining the driving power of a percussion section, particularly the rumble of low tom-toms.

PK

STEP BY STEP

Words and Music by
DAVID STRASSER
Arranged by Phillip Keveren

R.H. over L.H.

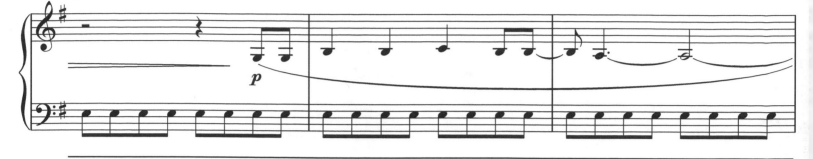